Plan Your
Dissertation

Sara Miller McCune founded SAGE Publishing in 1965 to support the dissemination of usable knowledge and educate a global community. SAGE publishes more than 1000 journals and over 800 new books each year, spanning a wide range of subject areas. Our growing selection of library products includes archives, data, case studies and video. SAGE remains majority owned by our founder and after her lifetime will become owned by a charitable trust that secures the company's continued independence.

Los Angeles | London | New Delhi | Singapore | Washington DC | Melbourne

SUPER
QUICK
SKILLS

Plan Your Dissertation

Charlotte Brookfield
Jamie Lewis

Los Angeles | London | New Delhi
Singapore | Washington DC | Melbourne

Los Angeles | London | New Delhi
Singapore | Washington DC | Melbourne

SAGE Publications Ltd
1 Oliver's Yard
55 City Road
London EC1Y 1SP

SAGE Publications Inc.
2455 Teller Road
Thousand Oaks, California 91320

SAGE Publications India Pvt Ltd
B 1/I 1 Mohan Cooperative Industrial Area
Mathura Road
New Delhi 110 044

SAGE Publications Asia-Pacific Pte Ltd
3 Church Street
#10-04 Samsung Hub
Singapore 049483

Editor: Jai Seaman
Editorial assistant: Hannah Cavender-Deere
Production editor: Victoria Nicholas
Marketing manager: Catherine Slinn
Cover design: Shaun Mercier
Typeset by: C&M Digitals (P) Ltd, Chennai, India

Library of Congress Control Number: 2021946916

British Library Cataloguing in Publication data

A catalogue record for this book is available from the
British Library

ISBN 978-1-5297-9082-5 (pbk)

Contents

Everything in this book!

Section 1   What is a dissertation?

This section outlines the purpose and general structure of a social science dissertation. It also describes how a dissertation differs from other forms of assessment that you have undertaken.

Section 2   Is a dissertation for me?

This section discusses the skill sets that are developed and refined when undertaking a dissertation. It covers issues such as time management, expectations, and how best to make use of the resources you have available.

Section 3   How do I pick my research topic?

This section highlights key sources of inspiration when choosing a research topic for a dissertation. Principally, it stresses the importance of coming up with a doable and manageable project.

Section 4   What is the role of the supervisor in the dissertation?

This section outlines what the role of the dissertation supervisor entails. It includes tips and suggestions for how to work effectively with your supervisor.

Section 5   How do I manage my time effectively?

This section includes hints and tips to help you effectively plan your time to ensure that you complete your dissertation on time and to a high standard.

Section 6   What do I need to read before I start?

This section helps you identify existing literature in your research area. It highlights some key subject-specific journals and introduces Boolean search terms.

Section 7   How do I produce an ethically sensitive piece of research?

This section underscores the importance of carefully considering the ethical issues associated with a research project from the outset. It helps you think about planning an ethically sensitive project.

Section 8   What methods should I use?

This section discusses the range of methods available to you to conduct a dissertation research project. It stresses the importance of choosing the most appropriate method(s) to address your research question(s).

What is a dissertation?

10 second
summary

A dissertation is an extended piece of
writing usually reporting the findings of
an independent piece of research and
completed under the supervision of a
member of academic staff.

A dissertation is a coherent piece of writing divided into several well-defined chapters. For undergraduates, a dissertation usually ranges between 8,000 and 10,000 words, and for postgraduates between 12,000 and 20,000 words. It is completed towards the end of your degree programme and is an opportunity to showcase the skills and knowledge that you have developed in taught modules.

There is significant breadth in the range of topics you may choose to research, which can be approached using a variety of different methods. These include both quantitative and qualitative approaches, as well as primary data collection and secondary data analysis. Importantly, dissertations need to be ethically sensitive and doable projects.

While a dissertation is an independent piece of work, you will be supported throughout by an academic tutor or supervisor.

Introduction

Dissertations offer exciting prospects in which you are afforded the opportunity to develop your thinking on topics and concepts that have interested you most during your degree programme. Typically, a dissertation is an extended piece of writing in which you produce a piece of independent research. This often involves the presentation of findings to address a set of research questions posed by you on a topic of your choosing. The project is a substantial piece of work and brings together the research skills that you have acquired during your university journey: organizational skills, research design skills, analytical skills, and writing skills.

Reflecting the work involved in producing a polished dissertation, the dissertation module is usually weighted higher than other modules, and, for most students, will be the longest single piece of writing you have been assessed on. Producing a coherent piece of work in which each chapter transitions well from the previous one while at the same time working as standalone sections can be a challenge, and a daunting one at that. The word count might seem overwhelming to begin with but breaking down the dissertation into individual chapters and sections should make it more manageable. In this sense, it might be beneficial to think of the dissertation as a series of smaller tasks and chapters.

Structure of a dissertation

Dissertations have a rhythm; they have logic, and they have a recognisable structure. That is, while, importantly, there is no one way to present a dissertation, most tend to broadly follow the structure of:

- Introduction

- Literature review

Introduction

The first chapter in a dissertation. It tells the reader what the research problem or topic of focus is and the importance of researching in this area. It also outlines the overall structure of the dissertation.

- Methods

- Findings

- Data analysis

- Conclusion

- With the dissertation bookended by a short abstract and a detailed reference list.

It is, however, perfectly acceptable to tinker with this outline: many dissertations, for example, will combine the findings and analysis chapters into a longer discussion chapter. What is important though is that the finished dissertation has a start, a middle, and an end.

Literature review
A chapter in a dissertation that synthesizes the existing literature in the field. This critical review of the literature should lead to the development and refinement of research questions.

Methods chapter
A chapter in a dissertation that describes the methodological approach adopted for the research. It should include details of the advantages and disadvantages of the chosen method for exploring your research topic.

Findings chapter
A chapter in a dissertation that reports and presents your main findings. This might come in tabular, chart or text form.

Data analysis chapter
A chapter in a dissertation that presents the analysis of data.

Conclusion
The final chapter in a dissertation. It summarizes the research, highlights the strengths and limitations of the research, and puts forward suggestions for future research.

Reference list
At the end of your dissertation you should include a reference list which lists in alphabetical order all the references cited in the main body of the text.

Abstract
A brief summary of the dissertation. It is positioned at the beginning of the document and is written to help the reader get an idea of the purpose and contents of the work to follow.

Discussion chapter
A chapter in a dissertation that brings together the main findings from your research with existing literature in the field.

Three-part mantra

It is important to tell the reader what you are going to do (this tends to include the introduction and literature review chapters), do it (this tends to involve the methods chapter but also possibly the findings chapter) and then say what you have done (this tends to include the analysis and conclusion chapters). Of course, there is much more to a social science dissertation than this but remembering this three-part simple mantra (see Figure 1) will hopefully encourage you to foreshadow and signpost throughout, providing a coherent thread that pulls together your write-up.

Figure 1   Three-part mantra

Dissertations as doable projects

As a student, you get the opportunity to shape your own research, to formalize your curiosity, and to produce the type of knowledge detailed in the many books and journals you have read at university. But you are not alone on this quest. While what you produce is an independent piece of work, you will likely be allocated a supervisor or tutor at the beginning of the module who will be a source of support, mentorship, and guidance throughout. With your supervisor, you will refine your broad project outline into a doable and ethically sensitive project, one that can be completed within the timeframe given.

In many ways, as a social science student, you have a blank canvass (though some programmes have a set of guidelines on what you should focus your topic on). The 'social' can be found everywhere, from the most mundane activities such as household chores to extraordinary,

Supervisor
The academic mentor that you have been allocated who will help, guide, and monitor your process throughout the lifecycle of the dissertation.

once in a generation events such as the COVID-19 pandemic, but narrowing the focus into a workable and sensible project is a key component of research design. While there is absolutely nothing wrong with thinking big, being enthusiastic, being ambitious, it is also important to recognize some of the constraints at play when planning a dissertation. These might include:

- Ethical issues

- Access difficulties

- Time constraints

- Cost implications

- Word count.

Here, it is worth emphasizing that the dissertation is the finished written project, but a lot of work that gets you to that point remains hidden or invisible. Writing within a word count means you will have to cut out significant bits of work, work that has taken you time and effort. Simply put, reducing a well-designed research product down to a word count is itself a job that involves significant synthesizing skills. This work and these words are not redundant though. They are part of the process of writing a tightly crafted piece of work.

That is, importantly, a dissertation is a process: things will need to be refined and unanticipated challenges might appear. This is all part of the dynamism, of the rough and tumble, of doing research. When planning a dissertation, always expect the unexpected and factor in time for things to go wrong. With good time management, you can make it right later.

CHECK LIST What is a dissertation?

Use the following checklist to evaluate your own understanding of what a dissertation is:

☐ I know what is involved in a dissertation.

☐ I am aware that a dissertation is an independent piece of work.

☐ I understand that a dissertation builds on the foundational work taught in other modules.

☐ I am aware that I need to design a doable, manageable project that can be completed in the time allowed.

☐ I understand that I will work closely with a supervisor who is there for support and guidance throughout my dissertation journey.

A student asked us

'Is a dissertation different to an essay?'

Compared to other academic essays, a dissertation tends to be a longer piece of work drawing from a research project that you have conducted. It is divided into several chapters, which often include an introduction, literature review, methods, findings, analysis, and conclusion chapters. The literature review chapter is most closely aligned to a standard essay, in the sense that you are building an argument by drawing on relevant academic literature; however, importantly you are funnelling into your own research project. Undoubtedly, some of the writing and referencing skills that you have learnt previously while writing essays will be important in crafting a dissertation.

'Say what you are going to do, do it, and then say what you have done.'

ACTIVITY Read a completed dissertation

Read a completed dissertation! As module convenors, we ask students from previous years if we can store an anonymized copy of their dissertation for the next cohort to read. As a student preparing to do a dissertation you should read one such dissertation, not simply for substantive content but also for how it is structured. In particular, consider how the student:

- Has introduced a topic

- Builds an argument

- Transitions to the next point

- Concludes the section.

It is also useful to choose a dissertation to read that has used methods or an approach similar to how you anticipate conducting your research. Look at:

- How the student has presented their data

- How the student has discussed their methodological approach

- The constraints on what the student can say.

Use the space provided below to make any notes:

....

....

....

Is a dissertation
for me?

*10 second
summary*

Completing a dissertation enables you
to develop your research, writing, and
analysis skills. Being proactive and
disciplined will go a long way in ensuring
you can complete your dissertation
on time.

The dissertation module is somewhat different to other taught modules. While the module is likely to be scaffolded by a series of lectures, workshops, and other drop-in sessions, there is an expectation that you are self-driven and proactive. This, however, does not mean that you are solely left to your own devices. A strong working relationship with your supervisor will ensure good and timely progress.

The dissertation provides an opportunity to explore a topic that interests you in more depth. This allows you to finesse your research, writing, and analysis skills.

In some institutions the dissertation is optional; in others, and on certain degree programmes, it is compulsory. It is worth checking whether a dissertation is a compulsory part of your degree programme early on in your course.

Introduction

We often get asked by students interested in doing a dissertation how the module differs to the other taught modules on offer. The undercurrent of this question is whether they are best suited to doing a dissertation and whether they have the skills required to complete one. It is important to stress here that in some institutions completing a dissertation (whether an empirical piece of work or an independent piece of scholarship) is compulsory. To graduate from these universities, a student will need to complete an independent piece of work. Even when the dissertation is not a requisite of a particular institution, it is also the case that certain programmes, such as those where you are attempting to obtain British Psychological Society (BPS) accreditation, require you to undertake a dissertation.

Hard skills

The hard skills that you will need to successfully complete your dissertation will vary according to the project and approach you are taking. You may need to develop skills in designing data collection tools such as surveys and interview schedules, data analysis, and writing in a concise and coherent manner. You will not necessarily have mastered these skills before taking the dissertation module. They are to be learnt and refined as part of the dissertation journey.

As with other taught modules, dissertation modules are assessed. They also do not exist in a vacuum, and you are not simply left to your own devices. Alongside an allocated supervisor or tutor you should also be supported by a range of lectures, seminars, drop-ins, and workshops all geared to help you achieve the best dissertation possible and to sharpen and harness your skills.

It is perhaps useful to think of the dissertation module as an extension or culmination of previous methodological and conceptual taught modules you have undertaken. For example, as a social science student, it is likely that you will have completed generic qualitative and quantitative training as well as undertaken more specialized methodological modules, such as ethnography, secondary data analysis, or focus groups. It is also likely you will have completed at least one social theory module. Here, you will have built up foundational knowledge that you can put into practice in your own independent research. We would always advocate that a student pursues an approach and a topic that they have enjoyed and/or are interested in. Choose a project that you already have lived experience of, or which builds on your strengths and the work and readings you have done previously. Here, then, you will already have a head start; you will have some understanding of the object that you want to research and, also likely, some knowledge of research in the area. This means you can begin sketching out project ideas, downloading relevant journal articles, and reading appropriate texts before the module starts. Important though, of course, is that you will need to receive a favourable decision from your department or school's ethics committee before you can embark on any data collection.

Qualitative research methods

A group of research methods such as interviews, observational techniques, and photo elicitation that is interested in meaning. Research involves an interpretivist, naturalistic approach to the subject at hand.

Quantitative research methods

A group of research methods such as surveys, experiments, and quantitative content analysis that result in numeric data which can be analysed using statistical approaches.

Beyond these research skills, there are also some soft skills that come in handy to make the best out of being an independent learner. At the start of the module, it might feel like you have everything and nothing to do. Convenors will be aware that students have different learning styles, working patterns, and their bespoke project will have its own rhythm too. For example, if you are collecting data yourself, access issues will determine when this starts. If you are using secondary data, you are not constrained so much by this. So, as much as the module has a structure, there may be more flexibility built into the delivery and expected progress when compared to other taught modules. Therefore, we always tell students not to compare their progress with other students but to make sure you are hitting the individual timelines agreed between you and your supervisor.

Creating your own individual dissertation map or Gantt chart will help you keep on top of things. Therefore, in preparing to do a dissertation, students might wish to put more emphasis on their organizational skills. Create your own individual timetable that includes the formal timetabled

Gantt chart
A visual representation that outlines the length of time you plan to spend on different tasks and the order in which you will complete different tasks.

lectures and supervision but also slots for independent learning. Try to be as specific as possible with these slots. Do not simply call them 'independent learning' or 'dissertation work' – include what you are going to do, for example:

- Read paper by Singh et al. on school attendance during COVID

- Write section on epistemology and ontology

- Update my Endnote file.

But recognize that these timetables are live documents and can change due to competing deadlines, unforeseen circumstances, etc. By going into the module aware that this sort of timetabling discipline is important you will be able to keep on top of your individual progress and set tangible tasks which you can share with your supervisor.

Employability skills

It might also be worthwhile thinking about what you want to do in the future and thinking how the dissertation module might help prepare you for work. Showing that you have completed a dissertation can sometimes help with applying for jobs as you are able to evidence empirical, communication, and writing skills as well as project management. As well as employment in academia, many social science graduate jobs involve an element of research or evaluation, for example government research centres, charities, and educational organizations. Developing these employability skills whilst at university is likely to help you when transitioning to the world of work.

Is a dissertation for me?

Use the following checklist to help you consider whether a dissertation is for you:

 I know whether a dissertation is a compulsory component of my degree programme.

I know the skills I will learn on the dissertation module.

I am aware that I will need to be proactive and disciplined when working on my dissertation.

I have spoken to others who have completed a dissertation.

I have asked a member of staff my outstanding questions about completing a dissertation.

Am I a good fit for the dissertation module?

It can be worthwhile speaking to other people who have already completed a dissertation to ascertain whether it is a good option for you. This may include lecturers but also previous students and family and friends. Some universities will run module fairs where you can speak to students currently studying the dissertation module and to the module convenors.

'Think of the dissertation as an extension of your previous interests and learning.'

ACTIVITY Skills I want to develop

Using the spaces beneath the headings below, note the skills you most want to develop when undertaking your dissertation:

Hard skills (methodological skills, data analysis skills etc):

....

....

....

....

....

....

....

Soft skills (time management, editing skills, etc):

....

....

....

....

....

....

....

How do I pick my research topic?

10 second summary

It can be difficult to choose a topic to research. You may take inspiration from topics you have learnt about, events happening in the media, or even your own hobbies.

Choosing a research project for your dissertation can be exciting but also overwhelming. It is important to choose a topic that you are interested in. You also need to ensure that it is feasible to research your chosen topic. Inspiration for what to focus on may come from other taught modules, events occurring in the media, or even your own hobbies and interests.

We would advise that you check what, if any, parameters your university has concerning the topics which you are able to research. Degrees accredited by professional bodies, such as the British Psychological Society, will sometimes have requirements around the choice of topic.

Introduction

Choosing a research topic can be both an exciting and daunting prospect. Once decided it directs the rest of your dissertation. It is not unusual for students to be unsure or undecided on what they want to research, so do not get overly concerned. Preparation is key. We tend to advise students to begin thinking about what they want to do in advance of starting the module. Begin with a broad idea of what you want to study, what interests you, and then start refining the idea into a manageable, researchable project.

Sources of inspiration

There are a wide range of topics that you can research for your dissertation. Sources of inspiration for your dissertation may come from any of the following:

- Modules or topics you have previously studied

- Current events showcased in the media

- Events that you have experienced or are living through (e.g. COVID-19)

- People you know

- Career aspirations or plans

- Hobbies and interests.

We suggest picking a topic that you are interested in and keen to find out more about. It is inevitable that you will get a little frustrated with your dissertation at some point! However, you want to minimize these times and a good way to do this is to pick a topic to research that sustains your interest.

Factors to consider

While students often do have a lot of flexibility in choosing their dissertation topic, when planning your research, it is important to consider other factors such as time and resources which may impact on your ability to successfully research different topics. For example, while it may be really interesting to research a very elite, hard-to-reach group such as politicians, the practicalities of accessing these groups may be beyond the scope of your research.

Also, some degree programmes, especially those accredited by professional bodies, have guidance and parameters around dissertation topic choices. Therefore, when planning your dissertation, it is important to check whether there are any specific degree programme requirements concerning your chosen topic.

Overall, it is vital that when you plan your dissertation you choose a topic that you can realistically research. Effectively planning your time can help you determine what is feasible in the timeframe you have.

Knowing where to begin

The freedom over the choice of the topic of your dissertation research can mean that it is difficult to know where to begin. Because of this, it is essential that once you pick a topic you narrow down your focus and think carefully about how you will plan your time effectively to complete your dissertation on time and to a high standard. Narrowing down the focus of your research can be a tricky process. It is often a good idea to look at the existing literature in the field to establish what is and what is not already known about your chosen topic. This can help in finding a 'hook' into your research or identifying a way in which your research will be original as well as contributing to the existing literature.

How do I pick a topic?

Use the following checklist to help you consider whether you have identified an appropriate research topic for your dissertation:

 I have chosen a topic that I am excited to research for my dissertation.

I have checked whether there are any requirements concerning the topic I can research for my dissertation.

I have considered the feasibility of researching my chosen topic for my dissertation.

'It can be really hard to narrow down your focus.'

Students often begin the dissertation process with grand ideas for their research. However, often the scope of these projects is too large, especially given the narrow timeframe that you have to complete your dissertation. It is extremely important to think about how realistic your project is and whether it is doable in the time allocated. Often dissertations that are more modest in their scope are the most successful ones as students have sufficient time, resources, and skills to complete them!

'Think small and narrow.'

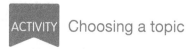

ACTIVITY Choosing a topic

Using the spaces beneath the headings below, consider in more detail the topic that you wish to focus on. Ask yourself:

- What is it you want to focus on?

- Why is it an important topic to study?

- How do you envisage studying the topic?

- Who will you need to engage with to research the topic?

- Where will you need to go to successfully research this topic?

Once you have completed this activity, share your suggestions with your supervisor. They will be able to help you assess the feasibility of your ideas.

What?

In general terms, explain what you want to focus on. What is the topic/ question of research that you are interested in? *It is perfectly acceptable to start big but also it is important to think about how you can make it specific and focused.*

....

....

....

....

....

Why?

Why is this an important project?

....

....

....

....

....

How?

How are you going to study your topic? Why is this the best approach?

....

....

....

....

....

Who?

Who will be involved in your research? Are there any key stakeholders or gatekeepers you need to consider?

....

....

....

....

Where?

Where will you undertake your research? Is this a safe space for both you and your participants?

....

....

....

....

....

Congratulations

You have now checked whether a dissertation is a required component of your course. If it is optional, you have thought through what a dissertation entails and whether it is likely to work for you. You have learnt that the dissertation is an extension or culmination of your previous work at university and that you need to think carefully about what it is you want to research and how that is achievable in the time you have.

The next sections consider the role of your supervisor and the importance of managing your time.

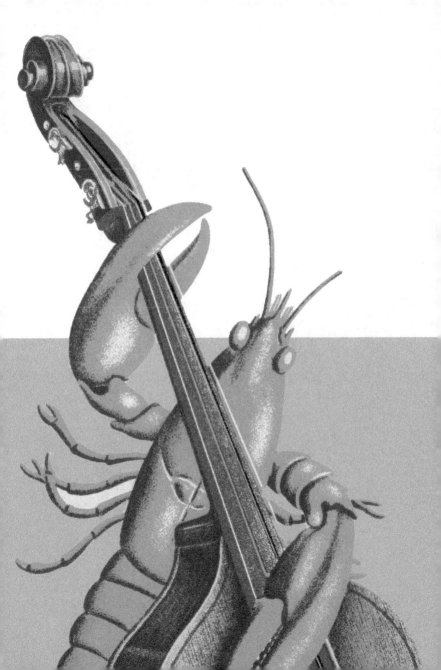

What is the role of the supervisor in the dissertation?

10 second
summary

As part of the dissertation module, you should be allocated a supervisor (sometimes called a tutor). They are there to guide you through the lifecycle of the project by making helpful suggestions.

60 second
summary

When doing a dissertation, you are likely to get two central sources of support. The module convenors will provide more general guidance through the delivery of regular lectures and workshops, but this should be supplemented by meetings with your supervisor. It is useful to think of your supervisor as a mentor whose job it is to advise you on your progress.

It is a good idea for you to initiate and maintain contact with your supervisor on a regular basis and discuss all aspects of the research with them, from designing the project, ethics, data collection, through to the final write-up. It is essential to build a good relationship with your supervisor as they are the best source of information; ask questions, discuss nascent ideas, propose solutions.

Introduction

Students tend to find the dissertation module a slightly different experience compared to other taught modules. Due to its dynamic and idiosyncratic nature it can be less uniform insofar as students will progress with their dissertations at different speeds. To keep you on track, at the beginning of the project, you should be allocated an individual supervisor who is your first port of call to speak to about ideas or concerns. Your supervisor's job is to help you set realistic targets, to work with you to produce a timetable, and to ensure you strike an appropriate balance between research that is manageable, worthwhile, and interesting, but which also gives you the opportunity to develop your own skills and confidence.

How are supervisors allocated?

It is likely that your supervisor will be allocated more than one student and it may be the case that they hold group supervisory meetings. Supervisors tend to be allocated to students' projects based on their research interests and methodological expertise. That is, if you are doing an interview-based project, you might very well be allocated a supervisor who is well versed in qualitative methods. If you are doing a project involving schools, you could be allocated a supervisor from the education teaching team. Sometimes though it is not possible to allocate a like-for-like supervisor. One of us, for example, supervised a project on Wicca witches. You need not worry here; all supervisors will be experienced in research and very familiar with what a completed dissertation should look like. If there are specific questions that a supervisor is unsure of, there will be other sources of support such as the module convenors or other lecturing staff to lean on.

Supervisory meetings

It is essential that you are proactive in arranging supervisory meetings. You should meet up with your supervisor very early on in your dissertation process. You may be asked to initiate the first meeting by emailing them. In the first meeting, you should discuss your project idea, any questions you have, and how you imagine progressing. No supervisor should expect your idea to be refined yet, but the purpose of this initial meeting is to work through how the project might proceed and what needs finessing. It is therefore a very good idea to come prepared with initial thoughts. Think also about your expectations and ambitions and get across what you are interested in researching. You should emerge from your initial meeting with a clearer idea of what you are hoping to discover, a way of taking the research forward, as well as reflections on how the project can be sensitive to any ethical issues.

At the end of the supervisor meeting, set a date for the next meeting so you have it in the diary. Your supervisor might suggest one-to-one supervisory meetings, group supervisory meetings (with other students they are supervising), or a combination of both. These meetings might be done in person or online.

The supervisory relationship

The best supervisory meetings should be student-led in which you come to the meeting prepared to talk and discuss the work you have done. That is, these sessions are not didactic lectures in which the lecturer simply talks and instructs. Supervisory meetings should be a two-way street, so take the initiative. You should make sure that you use the sessions with the supervisor to support and guide you as much as possible. Everyone will handle the relationship between supervisor and student slightly differently, but make sure that however you manage the relationship, it works for you. The ideal is for you to be able to get on with your supervisor well enough to develop a working relationship that works well for both parties.

As a guide, you may want to follow these ideas for meetings with your supervisor.

- At your first meeting, agree the broad research strategy and begin refining and narrowing the project (at the end of the meeting it is a good idea to put a date in the diary for the next one).

- At the second meeting, come prepared to discuss ethical procedures and agree with your supervisor an overall work plan for the completion of the dissertation and a schedule of meetings.

- During the subsequent meetings, you should discuss all aspects of your project, from reading the literature, data collection, analysis, and finally to presenting and writing up your research. We would advise that each meeting be themed to discuss one aspect of your work, e.g. the methods chapter.

Clear and regular communication is central to a good supervisory relationship. Maintain regular contact with your supervisor, be sure to keep appointments, and alert them to any issues that have impeded your progress as soon as possible. Dates for next meetings can be changed, but it is vital that you alert your supervisor without delay. Finally, attend meetings prepared, ask questions, and pose alternatives if things are not working.

CHECK LIST

What happens in a supervisory meeting?

Use the following checklist to evaluate your understanding of the role of the supervisor in your dissertation journey and to ensure you are aware of your responsibilities in maintaining a good supervisory relationship:

☐ I understand what the role of the dissertation supervisor entails.

☐ I recognize that the onus is on me to arrange meetings with my supervisor.

☐ I know that I need to come to meetings organized and prepared to talk.

A student asked us

'Is my supervisor my only point of contact?'

Whilst your supervisor is your primary point of contact, there are various sources of support. These include module convenors, teaching staff, and other staff in your department. Having a supervisor does not preclude you from speaking to other members of academic staff who may have expertise or experience in your field of research. We would strongly advise though that you discuss this first with your supervisor as they will have an overview of your project and your progress.

'Supervision is a two-way street.'

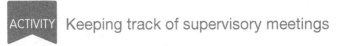

ACTIVITY Keeping track of supervisory meetings

Use the table below to keep track of discussions that you have in your supervisory meetings:

Table 1 Dissertation Meeting Log

Written dissertation: ....words

Introduction	Literature Review	Methods	Data Analysis and Interpretation	Discussion and Conclusions

Meeting Date:	Notes and Agreed Actions:

How do I manage
my time effectively?

*10 second
summary*

Dissertations take time to craft. Making the most of the time you have available by setting agreed intermediate deadlines with your supervisor and factoring in unforeseen delays is critical.

Planning your time effectively from the outset can ensure that you finish your dissertation on time and to a high standard. It is important to consider how long each part of the dissertation will take, allowing time for any unforeseen delays, and for your supervisor to provide feedback on your work.

It is necessary to think carefully about how you will balance your time effectively across all the modules that you are studying alongside your dissertation. Writing for your dissertation on a frequent basis can help with this.

It is easy to underestimate the time scales of a dissertation. Speaking with your supervisor about how best to use your time can be extremely helpful. Set agreed deadlines with your supervisor and create a Gantt chart to help manage your time.

Introduction

To undertake a dissertation effectively, you need to manage your time efficiently. The process of completing a dissertation does not necessarily mirror the structure of a final, completed dissertation. Think of writing a dissertation like completing a jigsaw. While it is usual to begin working on a literature review chapter, the introductory chapter which precedes this is often one of the last chapters to be written. Here, keeping on top of what you have included in certain chapters and the time needed to go back to edit, move around, and integrate is key to good time management. This is where having a separate live document tracking the progress of your dissertation might help you manage this effectively. It is also likely to be the case that you will be working on multiple chapters at the same time or that you will be writing sections of your dissertation alongside collecting or analysing data. Again, this underscores the importance of carefully planning your time at the outset of your dissertation.

Key dates for your diary

Usually, a dissertation will have a higher word count than other assessments in different modules. This inevitably means that it takes longer to complete. It is also likely to include a phase of data collection and/or data analysis. Therefore, it is important to plan your time effectively to ensure that you can complete your dissertation on time. As part of the planning process, you should find out the following key dates:

- The dissertation deadline (the date and time you need to hand in the final version of your dissertation)

- The date that you need to submit your research idea to your university's research ethics committee

- Dates and times of meetings with your supervisor

- Dates for any other assessments within the dissertation module, for example a presentation component.

It is also worth remembering that alongside the dissertation, you will often have assessment deadlines for other modules that you are studying. Therefore, in the planning stages, it can be useful to make note of these key dates to ensure sufficient time to focus on these assessments. You do not want to be conducting interviews for your dissertation on the same day as a big test.

Depending on the setting of the research, it may also be necessary to think about whether there are any other key times to avoid when planning fieldwork. For example, if you are hoping to interview secondary school students about their career aspirations, it would be sensible to avoid exam periods when schools are unlikely to grant you access to undertake your research. Being mindful of these dates at the outset of a research project can help avoid delays later.

It is also important to factor in sufficient time for your supervisor to read and comment on drafts of your work. It is worthwhile agreeing early on in the dissertation journey, dates that you will send your supervisor work. Remember that your supervisor may be supervising more than one student, so it is essential that they are able to block out time in their diary to read your work and provide you with valuable feedback.

Writing is an iterative process

Writing a dissertation is an iterative process. This means that it is very likely that you will have to draft and redraft your work. Therefore, it is important that you start writing your dissertation as soon as possible. We always encourage our students to get the dissertation written first and get it right after. Feel free to begin writing without constraint and then refine and edit later. The article you read in a journal is never the author's first draft.

The best dissertations are the ones that have had time to breathe, that have been crafted, and re-crafted. That is, dissertations involve a cyclical process of refinement and tweaking. Recognizing that this is the process early on, before you embark on the dissertation, sets realistic expectations as to the work involved in producing the final text. Often you will end up writing many more words than will be in your final dissertation. For this reason, it is important that when you plan your dissertation you factor in time towards the end to edit.

Writing up is a craft that can be improved upon. We therefore also encourage students considering writing a dissertation to begin playing with their ideas early on, turning them into full sentences, into nascent arguments that they can finesse as they proceed.

Unforeseen delays

Despite careful planning, unforeseen or unexpected delays sometimes occur in the research process. For example, a participant may become unwell and be unable to take part in the research or access may not run smoothly. Equally, circumstances in your life may at times prevent you from being able to carry out your research and write your dissertation. Remember, your health and well-being comes first and foremost. It is, therefore, a good idea to build in some extra time when planning how long you intend to spend on each part of the dissertation.

It is important, if you do encounter unexpected delays to your work, that you let your supervisor know. Your supervisor will be able to offer practical advice and support in these circumstances. They may suggest a workaround that will enable you to progress with your research and, if necessary, they can help you find out more about your institution's processes for applying for extensions.

Gantt charts

A good way to help organize your time is to agree some intermediary deadlines with your supervisor. It can be useful to get these in the diary when you are planning your dissertation. Having these mini deadlines to work towards can help you maintain momentum with your research and help ensure you finish on time.

A Gantt chart is a visual representation of how long you plan to spend on each task and the order in which you plan to undertake each activity. It can be helpful to create a Gantt chart at the beginning of the module. Figure 2 shows an example Gantt chart.

Figure 2   An example Gantt chart

CHECK LIST Recording key dates

Use the following checklist to make sure that you have all key dates recorded in your diary. This will help you stay on track when you start your dissertation.

 I know the deadline date for my dissertation.

 I am aware of when I need to apply for ethical approval for my dissertation.

 I have taken into account the deadlines for other module assessments.

 I have agreed some intermediary deadlines with my supervisor.

 I have produced a Gantt chart for my dissertation.

Use the space below to write down key dates and deadlines:

....

....

....

....

....

....

....

'Never underestimate the time it takes to format
your dissertation.'

Students have repeatedly told us that they are surprised at the length of time it takes to proofread and format their dissertations (adding page numbers, creating a table of contents, and writing a reference list). Make sure that you factor in sufficient time for these final tasks. While they are often the elements of the dissertation that you finish last, they are still very important to the overall look of the final dissertation. We suggest you set yourself an internal deadline at least a week before the official deadline so that you have the time to edit.

'Get it written first, then get it
right after.'

Managing your time

Using the table on the next page (Table 2), list all the key tasks you need to undertake to complete your dissertation (for example, literature review, collecting data, and analysing data). Give each task a start date and indicate how long it will take to complete.

Make sure that you show this table to your supervisor. They will be able to provide feedback on whether you have allocated sufficient time for each of the different sections of the research process and whether you have missed off any important tasks.

Table 2   Key Tasks for my Dissertation

Tasks:	Start Date:	Number of Days:

This table can be used to help you create a Gantt chart in Microsoft Excel.

Congratulations

You have learnt the value of managing your time and your supervisor. You have learnt that while a dissertation is an independent piece of work and you need to be self-driven and disciplined, there are sources of support available to you throughout the lifecycle of the project. Foremost of these is your allocated supervisor. Making these supervisory sessions work for you means coming prepared to the meetings and keeping on top of your agreed targets and deadlines. You have also learnt that dissertations need to be crafted and involve a process of writing and rewriting, drafting, and redrafting.

The next three sections consider the importance of producing an ethically sensitive, methodologically robust project that is located in relevant literature.

What do I need to read before I start?

10 second summary

Research should be grounded in relevant literature. This includes academic literature published in journals and books, research reports, textbooks, professional literature, websites, and other publications including podcasts or news reports.

60 second summary

Reading relevant literature will help refine the focus of the project. Specifically, literature can be useful for identifying knowledge gaps existing in the field. Engaging with literature should also help you think about different ways in which you can research your chosen topic and some of the advantages and disadvantages of using different methods.

There are various sources of literature. Academic literature (journal articles and academic books) is generally considered the most credible for research projects. This is because most academic manuscripts are themselves drawn from research which has undergone a robust peer-review process.

Library and individual journal databases, as well as Google Scholar, can be good places to start looking for literature. Boolean search terms help refine your literature searches.

Introduction

Most dissertations will contain a literature review chapter. This is where you will summarize and critique the existing studies concerning your research topic. You may decide to organize your account of the existing literature thematically, chronologically, or in terms of specificity. However you decide to organize your literature in your final dissertation, it is important that you begin to engage with existing studies early on in the dissertation process and locate your project within a body of work. Reading widely around your topic enables you to evaluate the need and originality of your research and will also provide you with ideas about how you can research your chosen topic. However, it can be difficult to choose what literature to read.

Sources of literature

There are various sources of literature that you may engage with as part of your preparatory reading for your dissertation. These include:

- Research literature (academic books and journal articles)

- Grey literature (research reports)

- Professional literature (publications for practitioners)

- Web publications

- Textbooks

- Other publications (e.g. TV, news, and podcasts).

Generally, research literature is considered the more valued and most credible source of literature. This is because research literature usually goes through a peer-review process

Peer review
The process of subjecting researchers' work to the scrutiny of other experts who assess the quality of the work.

before being published. This means that other academics within the field have rigorously evaluated and assessed the quality of the research. It is also because this literature often reports on findings drawn from research projects, themselves building on previous work. They thus provide a lineage for how ideas and concepts develop.

Other publications, including news articles, may be written from a particular perspective and for a different type of audience. It is important to be critical of the standpoint of different authors and to consider their motivations, political or otherwise, for writing their publications. This does not mean that other sources of literature should be excluded from your dissertation; however, it is likely that you will use these sources more sparingly and more as a 'hook' to underscore the importance, timeliness, and relevance of your research.

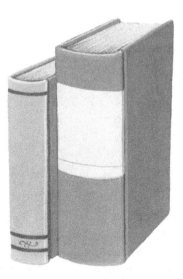

Social science journals

Table 3 highlights some of the key substantive journals in the social sciences.

Table 3   Suggested Substantive Social Science Journals

Suggested Substantive Journals
General Sociology
British Journal of Sociology
Sociology
Sociological Review
General Criminology
The British Journal of Criminology
Criminology and Criminal Justice
Criminology
General Education
Sociology of Education
British Educational Research Journal
British Journal of Educational Studies
General Psychology
British Journal of Psychology
British Journal of Social Psychology
General Social Policy
Journal of Social Policy
Social Policy and Society

There is also a tranche of more specific journals, for example (i) *Youth and Society*, (ii) *Race and Class*, (iii) *Time and Society*, (iv) *Big Data and Society*, (v) *Journal of Happiness Studies*, (vi) *Social Studies of Science*. As well as looking at substantive literature, it is important that you also consider relevant methodological literature. Your supervisor should be able to help direct you to relevant journals. Table 4 contains some suggestions of methods journals which you may wish to look at.

Table 4   Suggested Methodological Journals

Suggested Methodological Journals
General
International Journal of Social Research Methodology
Methodology
Quantitative
Social Science Research
Survey Research Methods
Qualitative
Qualitative Research
Qualitative Inquiry
Ethnography
Mixed Methods
Journal of Mixed Methods Research
International Journal of Quantitative and Qualitative Research Methods

Finding literature

Google Scholar is a search engine specifically for academic literature. There are also library databases, such as Web of Science, that you can use to search for academic literature.

Boolean search terms enable you to narrow down your literature search. This means that the results of your search are more relevant to your project. Below shows how Boolean search terms can be used in a literature search:

Boolean search terms
A series of terms that can be used to refine your literature search. These include "", 'AND', 'OR', and 'NOT'.

" " – ExactPhrase

AND – Must include both search terms

OR – Broadens search to include multiple search terms

NOT – Excludes specific search terms

For example, if you are interested in researching the impacts of COVID-19 on social science university students' learning you could use Boolean search terms in the following way:

"impacts on learning" – Results all include the phrase **impacts on learning**. By putting the phrase inside double quotation marks the search result will contain the exact phrase.

COVID-19 AND university – Results all include the terms **COVID-19** and **University.**

Sociology OR Criminology – Broadens search to include **Sociology** and **Criminology** students.

NOT school – Excludes results which include the term **school.**

CHECK LIST Engaging with literature

Use the following checklist to help ensure you have engaged with the most relevant literature for your dissertation.

☐ I have looked at a range of different sources of literature.

☐ I have considered potential biases in existing literature.

☐ I have searched discipline-specific journals.

☐ I have searched methodological journals.

☐ I have used Boolean search terms to refine my literature searches.

'It can sometimes feel like you are drowning
in literature.'

Students can be overwhelmed by the number of results a single literature search can return. This is why it is important to use Boolean search terms carefully to narrow down your literature search. Other criteria such as deciding to initially focus on more contemporary research studies published within the last ten years, for instance, can also be a good way in which to focus your search. Looking at literature that is frequently referenced by other authors will also give you a good insight into the studies that are most influential in your field of research.

'Read critically; select critically.'

Effective reading and note taking

Using Table 5 below will help you make effective notes and begin to think critically when reading.

Table 5   Effective Reading and Note Taking

Reference:
One sentence summary:
Main arguments/key claims:
Methods/data used:

Key conclusions:

Strengths and weaknesses:

How can I use this reading in my dissertation?

How do I produce
an ethically sensitive
piece of research?

*10 second
summary*

All research should be ethically sensitive.
This means minimizing risks to yourself as
a student researcher, to the participants in
the project, and to the university that you
represent.

All universities should have an ethics committee whose job is to assess the ethical sensitivity of your research project. You will need to have a favourable decision from the committee before you can proceed with data collection.

It is important that when designing a doable project you consider its ethical implications; Ethics committees are not designed to prevent you from doing research; their role is to help you think about how to mitigate harms and risks to your participants, you as a researcher, and to the university.

Importantly, ethics is not simply procedural form filling and does not simply concern data collection. Ethics is a process and it is pivotal to consider ethics from initial research design through to the write-up of your dissertation.

Introduction

Before proceeding with data collection, you will need a favourable decision from your school or departmental ethics committee. This is not something to be concerned about, but it is something to take seriously and will likely improve your research. This is not exclusive to students either; anyone conducting research, lecturing staff included, will need ethical clearance before embarking on research. Essentially, the procedure involves completing a form, which will be assessed by a group of academics (and possibly some lay persons too). These forms tend to have a uniform structure and will ask you:

- to detail your project

- to include your research questions

- how you intend to collect data

- who your participants are

- how you plan to recruit your participants

- where you plan to undertake your research

- whether participants are able to withdraw from the study

- about consent and confidentiality

- about data storage and security.

Ethics committee
The body responsible for ensuring that research projects are ethically sensitive, mitigating harm and risk.

Confidentiality
Involves a set of procedures or rules that keep ideas and/or identities private. Here the researcher should keep a confidence between them and their participants by not sharing with anyone full transcripts or audio recordings.

Ultimately then, the ethical approval form provides you with the opportunity to get detailed plans of your project down on paper early on in the project. Take time crafting your application and work with your supervisor on aspects that you are unsure about. Usually, the application needs to be signed off by your supervisor before you can submit it for review.

Institutional ethics

It is likely that your university has a code of conduct for doing research as well as guidance on safety in fieldwork/lone research. Your school or department should also have a collection of draft consent forms and information sheet templates that you can look at. The relevant professional organizations, such as the British Sociological Association (BSA), the

British Psychological Society (BPS), and the British Educational Research Association (BERA), will also have guidance on best practice. Do not shy away from highlighting the ethical challenges present in your project. Assessors will not be expecting a project to have no ethical concerns; instead they will want you to think through what risks and harms your project raises to both you and your participants, and what procedures and measures you intend to put in place to mitigate and control these. Once assessed by the committee, you will get a response. This might include the committee asking for further information or clarification or raising issues that you have not thought about. This is not unusual and again is not something to get overly concerned about. They will likely ask you to resubmit the form with amendments.

When considering your project, it is also important to be aware of other institutional policies and organizations' ethics committees. For example, some NHS projects where you recruit patients through the NHS require NHS REC (Research Ethics Committee) approval. This procedure sits outside the university and can be an extremely lengthy process, which ultimately means a project of this type would not fit within the timelines of an undergraduate dissertation. This does not mean that you cannot do a project on, for example, patients' experiences of living with chronic illness. If you recruit participants from an online support group and not through the NHS then the project will only be required to be assessed by your school or department.

Thus, it is the way in which you recruit participants that determines which ethics board you need to go through. Of course, many of the ethical considerations will be the same, and you will still need to consider carefully how you would design such a project. Some other organizations, such as charities, also have their own ethics procedures and you would need a favourable decision from both the university and the organization before conducting the research.

Other details to consider include the age of your participants. For example, if you are doing one-to-one research or other unsupervised research with children and young people under the age of 18, another consideration may be whether you are required to have an up-to-date criminal record and barred list check before commencing the research. Some other projects might simply be off limits for undergraduate students, for example with adults who do not have the capacity to consent, or a project that involves Her Majesties Prison and Probation Service (HMPPS).

Situational ethics

Importantly, while ethics has become increasingy institutionalized, you should not view it as simply procedural. Though various professional codes of ethics have been described above, it is important to reflect on your ethical positioning and value judgements *in situ*. Research settings are dynamic and situations might occur that you had not foreseen or anticipated. Ethics is then a process. It is not the case that once

Situational ethics
Situational ethics recognizes that the research field is dynamic and thus ethics needs to be flexible as well. Its position is that prescriptive ethics will not work in all situations and the researcher must be alive to ethical issues that arise *in situ*.

you have received a favourable decision from the committee that you are conducting ethical research. You need to be responsive and adaptive to situations which may arise during your research. There is no textbook here on how to act and react but building an ethical relationship with your participants is essential. If a situation does arise that you or your participants feel is particularly uncomfortable you might need to halt the fieldwork. While principally ethics is about exploring and minimizing risks to your participants, to yourself, and to the university, some situations have a complex array of conflicting interests. Speaking to your supervisor, who is likely to have more experience of these situations, is essential. Between the two of you it may even be the case that you include an addendum in the ethics application. Remember this is all good material for your methods chapter.

Ethics as a lifecycle

Finally, as ethically sensitive researchers you should consider ethical implications throughout the lifecycle of the project, from the planning and research design stage of the project through to the dissmination process and how you represent your participants in print. At the beginning of the project, consider how you could promote a culture of ethical reflection and continued learning.

CHECK LIST Producing an ethical piece of research

Use the following checklist to help ensure you plan and produce an ethically sensitive piece of research.

 I am aware that I will need to get a favourable decision from the ethics committee before collecting data.

 I am aware of the various professional bodies' codes of practice.

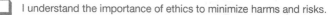 I understand the importance of ethics to minimize harms and risks.

 I recognize that ethics is a process and covers the lifecycle of the project.

I understand the differences between procedural or institutional ethics and personal or situational ethics.

A student
asked us

'When can I begin my data collection?'

Some students are keen to get started with their dissertation even before their final year has officially begun. However, it is really important that you do not start collecting data until you have received a favourable decision from your university or school ethics committee. If you are enthusiastic about starting your dissertation then we would advise you to read relevant literature and to consider and write down the ethical issues that might arise in your project.

'Ethics should be considered throughout the lifecycle of the project.'

ACTIVITY Planning ethically sensitive research

Using Table 6 below, answer the questions provided. Addressing these questions will help you consider the essential information that you will need to include on a university ethics committee application form.

Anonymity
Describes a situation where the person's identity is obscured or unknown and is thus untraceable.

Table 6   Planning Ethically Sensitive Research

1. Provide a **concise** overview of your research project stating the project's research questions.
2. Who are the research participants and how will they be recruited to the project?

3. How will you collect your data?

4. Where will you conduct your research?

5. How will you obtain, record, and maintain informed consent from research participants?

6. Will you anonymize data collected from your participants? Please explain how you propose to anonymize data.

7. Describe how you will mitigate possible harms to yourself or participants.

8. Detail how you will deal with data security and data storage.

What methods should I use?

10 second
summary

It is imperative that you choose the most appropriate method(s) to address your research question(s). You should also carefully consider the resource and time implications of various methodological approaches.

Choosing a research method requires you to consider the advantages
and disadvantages of different approaches and to carefully assess which
approach enables you to answer your research question(s) most effectively.

As well as picking a method that is methodologically robust, you must also
assess how doable the project is. This means thinking carefully about some
of the practical time and resource constraints that affect your research.

Mixed methods research tends to involve the employment of both
qualitative and quantitative approaches to studying your chosen topic.
However, we maintain that students should be cautious about utilizing more
than one method in their dissertation. This is because it can be difficult
in the timeframe allocated to carry out both methods effectively and report
the findings in a succinct and integrated fashion.

Introduction

An important milestone in planning your dissertation is deciding what method(s) to use. In the first instance, you should consider whether you want to collect your own data (primary data collection) or whether there is already sufficient data on your chosen topic that you could analyse or present in a new way (secondary data analysis). You also need to decide whether you will work with quantitative (numerical) or qualitative (textual or image-based) data. In some cases, it may be that you consider using more than one method in your dissertation. This approach is known as mixed methods research.

The research methods commonly used in social science dissertations include:

- Interviews
- Surveys
- Focus groups
- Observational techniques
- Secondary data analysis
- Analysis of documents.

Primary data collection
Data that are collected by the researcher first-hand and directly from participants.

Secondary data analysis
Analysing data that has been collected previously by other researchers or for different purposes. The UK Data Service has lots of existing quantitative and qualitative datasets freely available for you to download and analyse.

Mixed methods research
A research project that utilizes more than one method to investigate the topic of interest.

Answering your research question

Crucially, your chosen method should allow you to answer the research question(s) you have posed. Put simply, 'Why?' and 'How?' questions are usually answered using qualitative approaches, while 'Who?' and 'What?' questions can typically be answered using quantitative approaches. The research question should inform the chosen method and not the other way round. This means, for instance, if you are interested in understanding how social science students' learning has been impacted during the COVID-19 pandemic, you would be more likely to use qualitative approaches to ascertain the different ways in which students believed their learning had been affected. Meanwhile, if you were interested in finding out which students believed their learning had been impacted by the COVID-19 pandemic, you may choose to design and distribute a quantitative survey to identify who believed their learning had been impacted.

Time, resource, and expertise

While we encourage students to think very carefully about the type of method that best lends itself to their research question(s) at the planning stage of a dissertation, it is important to be mindful of project constraints. These include time and resource constraints as well as limits in your own expertise. For example, while it may be a nice idea to undertake a longitudinal study interviewing new mothers for the first ten years of their child's life, this project is simply not doable in the timeframe of a dissertation. Similarly, while you may read studies that have introduced interventions, for instance in educational settings, it is unlikely that you will have the access or knowledge and experience to undertake such a large-scale research project for your dissertation.

Equally, while it is important that you consider your research question(s) when choosing your research method, it is also essential to consider your participants. The method you use must effectively capture the abilities and capabilities of your sample.

Likert scale

A type of survey question where respondents have to indicate their level of agreement with a statement from 'strongly agree' to 'strongly disagree'.

For example, it might be unwise to use an online method to interview older people in a care home or people who live off grid who may not have access to technologies. Likewise, you may not want to use a standard Likert scale in a survey aimed at young children and instead decide to use a pictorial scale.

The online possibilities

Researching online presents a lot of new and exciting opportunities for social researchers. For example, the use of video call technology enables you to interview people who are geographically dispersed and could even be on the other side of the world to you. Equally, online survey software makes it easy to design and distribute surveys online. This software usually has the functionality to automatically transfer data to a spreadsheet and code responses. This can save an enormous amount of time when doing a research project. It is therefore always useful to familiarize yourself with the latest technologies and computer programs.

However, as with any approach to research, it is important when planning your project to be mindful of the potential challenges or limitations of researching online. It is also necessary to consider the ethical implications of undertaking your research in a virtual/online space as opposed to face to face. On the one hand, being able to participate in research from the comfort of their own homes can be a real benefit for some participants; however, it might be much harder, or in some cases impossible, to notice if a participant is becoming distressed by the research. Where and how data are saved on these online platforms is also important to understand.

Secondary data analysis

As an alternative to collecting your own data, you may decide to utilize pre-existing data. There is a wealth of data that is freely accessible to social researchers to analyse. The UK Data Service, for example, is home to various quantitative and qualitative datasets which you are able to freely download and analyse. This includes data collected by individual academics as part of their own research as well as data from large, nationwide surveys. Other places to access secondary sources of data include:

- The Office for National Statistics – www.ons.gov.uk

- Eurostat – https://ec.europa.eu/eurostat

- Data.gov.uk – https://data.gov.uk

- World Bank Open Data – https://data.worldbank.org

- SAGE Research Methods Datasets – https://methods.sagepub.com/datasets

It is important to stress that secondary data analysis involves the analysis of ready made datasets collected by others and deposited in their raw form (e.g. interview transcripts, survey data). This is different to collecting your own primary data from social media, newspapers, and TV programmes which you then go on to analyse.

Plan and pilot

It is always a good idea when planning your dissertation to allow plenty of time to engage with relevant methodological literature and any necessary training you may need. For example, when you have chosen a research method, you may find it helpful to do some extra reading around the method and/or to attend any additional training sessions or workshops run by your school or department. Some of these sessions might be focussed on method, and

Pilot study
A small study conducted in advance of research collection in which procedures, protocols, and instruments are tested. For example, you might test out your interview questions.

others on various types of software or computer programmes. Always leave time to become familiar with new technology.

Regardless of your chosen method, you should allocate time to pilot your chosen approach. A pilot study involves trialling your recruitment process, method, and analytic approach on a small(er) group of participants. The piloting process allows you to identify potential issues with your chosen method. For those students planning to undertake interviews, the piloting process can also be a way of gaining confidence in interviewing.

Choosing a method

Use the following checklist to help evaluate the appropriateness of your chosen method for your dissertation.

 I have used my research question(s) to guide the choice of method I will use in the dissertation.

 I have considered the strengths and limitations of my chosen method.

☐ I have thought about some of the ethical implications of my chosen method and planned ways to mitigate these.

'Will I get marked down for only using one
method?'

The short answer to this question is 'No, not at all!'. Often students falsely believe that by utilizing more than one method in their project (doing mixed methods research) they will be able to access higher marks. Some students believe that by utilizing both quantitative and qualitative research methods in one project, the limitations of each approach will cancel each other out. However, this is not necessarily the case. It can also be difficult to find sufficient time to properly collect and analyse both sources of data and it can be tricky to succinctly, yet adequately, describe and report the findings from more than one method in the allocated word count. We suggest that you speak with your supervisor before deciding on using more than one method in your dissertation.

'Your choice of method should be guided by
what you want to achieve.'

Advantages and disadvantages of research methods

Using Table 7 below, consider the advantages and disadvantages of different research methods for your chosen research question. Some empty rows are provided to allow you to consider alternative methods which are not listed.

Table 7   Advantages and Disadvantages of Research Methods

Method	Advantages	Disadvantages	Suitable for my research question (Yes/No)
Surveys			
Interviews			
Secondary Data Analysis			

Observational Methods			
Focus Groups			

Congratulations

You have learnt that designing a doable, manageable project means designing a project that is sensitive to any ethical implications, that draws from an appropriate methodological approach and builds on and is located in academic literature. While a dissertation should have an element of originality, this can come in multiple forms: the approach taken, the way in which the topic has been analysed and/or the social scientific concepts discussed. There is therefore a balance to be struck between originality and recognizing the work that has come before.

Final checklist: How to know you are done

If you have worked through this book, you will be in a good position to start your dissertation.

To be sure, here is a final checklist:

You have:

1 Checked whether the dissertation is a compulsory element of your programme ☐

2 Considered the advantages and disadvantages of doing a dissertation ☐

3 Read through a previously completed dissertation ☐

4 Selected a research topic and thought about how
   to research it ☐

5 Identified key dates for the dissertation module ☐

6 Created a timeline or Gantt chart for your project ☐

7 Understood the role of the supervisor ☐

8 Practised using Boolean search terms to look
   for relevant literature ☐

9 Familiarized yourself with the ethical procedures you will
   need to go through before collecting data ☐

Now it is time to start planning your dissertation.

Further reading and resources

Balmer, A. and Murcott, A. (2017). The Craft of Writing in Sociology: Developing the Argument in Undergraduate Essays and Dissertations. Manchester: Manchester University Press.

An in-depth guide to constructing persuasive arguments in the social sciences. The book includes tips on how to read and write concisely and critically.

Brookfield, C. (2021). Using Microsoft Excel for Social Research. London: Sage Publications.

A book demonstrating how Microsoft Excel can be used to help at various stages of the research process, including guidance on how to create a Gantt chart in Microsoft Excel at the start of a project.

O'Leary, Z. (2021). The Essential Guide to Doing your Research Project, 4th edn. London: Sage Publications.

A detailed guide to the research process drawing on examples from the author's own experience of researching.

The SAGE Project Planner: https://methods.sagepub.com/project-planner

An online tool to guide you through the research process.

Thomas, G. (2017). How to Do Your Research Project. A Guide for Students, 3rd edn. London: Sage Publications.

An engaging, interactive book guiding you through the research process, with clear roadmaps and a range of activities for you to complete.

Glossary

Abstract   A brief summary of the dissertation. It is positioned at the beginning of the document and is written to help the reader get an idea of the purpose and contents of the work to follow.

Anonymity   Describes a situation where the person's identity is obscured or unknown and is thus untraceable.

Boolean search terms   A series of terms that can be used to refine your literature search. These include; **""**, **AND**, **OR**, and **NOT**.

Conclusion   The final chapter in a dissertation. It summarizes the research, highlights the strengths and limitations of the research, and puts forward suggestions for future research.

Confidentiality   Involves a set of procedures or rules that keep ideas and/or identities private. Here the researcher should keep a confidence between them and their participants by not sharing with anyone full transcripts or audio recordings.

Data analysis chapter A chapter in a dissertation that presents the main findings of the data analysis.

Discussion chapter A chapter in a dissertation that brings together the main findings from your research with existing literature in the field.

Ethics committee The body responsible for ensuring that research projects are ethically sensitive, mitigating harm and risk.

Findings chapter A chapter in a dissertation that reports and presents your main findings. This might come in tabular, chart or text form.

Gantt chart A visual representation that outlines the length of time you plan to spend on different tasks and the order in which you will complete different tasks.

Institutional ethics The focus here is on the institutional responsibility of the university. It describes the professional procedures put in place to ensure research is ethical, including creation of the ethics committee.

Introduction   The first chapter in a dissertation. It tells the reader what the research problem or topic of focus is and the importance of researching in this area. It also outlines the overall structure of the dissertation.

Likert scale   A type of survey question where respondents have to indicate their level of agreement with a statement from 'strongly agree' to 'strongly disagree'.

Literature review   A chapter in a dissertation that synthesizes the existing literature in the field. This critical review of the literature should lead to the development and refinement of research questions.

Methods chapter   A chapter in a dissertation that describes the methodological approach adopted for the research. It should include details of the advantages and disadvantages of the chosen method for exploring your research topic.

Mixed methods research   A research project that utilizes more than one method to investigate the topic of interest.

Peer review   The process of subjecting a researcher's work to the scrutiny of other experts who assess the quality of the work.

Pilot study   A small study conducted in advance of research collection in which procedures, protocols, and instruments are tested. For example, you might test out your interview questions.

Primary data collection   Data that is collected by the researcher first-hand and directly from participants.

Qualitative research methods   A group of research methods such as interviews, observational techniques, and photo elicitation that is interested in meaning. Research involves an interpretivist, naturalistic approach to the subject at hand.

Quantitative research methods A group of research methods such as surveys, experiments, and quantitative content analysis that result in numeric data which can be analysed using statistical approaches.

Reference list At the end of your dissertation you should include a reference list which lists in alphabetical order all the references cited in the main body of the text.

Secondary data analysis Analysing data that has been collected previously by other researchers or for different purposes. The UK Data Service has lots of existing quantitative and qualitative datasets freely available for you to download and analyse.

Situational ethics Situational ethics recognizes that the research field is dynamic and thus ethics needs to be flexible as well. Its position is that prescriptive ethics will not work in all situations and the researcher must be alive to ethical issues that arise *in situ*.

Supervisor The academic mentor that you have been allocated who will help, guide, and monitor your process throughout the lifecycle of the dissertation.

9 781529 790825